THE DURATION OF GRIEF

THE DURATION OF GRIEF

by
Liane Ellison Norman

**SMOKE AND
MIRRORS PRESS**

Smoke and Mirrors Press
2005

Smoke and Mirrors Press
1139 Wightman Street
Pittsburgh, PA 15217

FIRST EDITION

Designed by Todd Sanders

Printed in the United States of America

Library of Congress Control Number: 2005904679
ISBN 978-0-9709590-2-7

TABLE OF CONTENTS

II.

PREFACE

My child, Emily Norman Davidson, died of cancer at the age of 36. She was mother to Katie Rose, who was eight years old at the time. She was also a baroque violinist, one of the founding members of Pittsburgh-based Chatham Baroque.

One friend called this an "impossible loss," a description that struck a deep chord. I found that I—a writer nearly all my life—was without the words to try to understand an experience I could not—cannot—fathom. Then I found that poetry, which I had not attempted for over 40 years, worked for me better than my familiar medium—prose.

I made a limited edition of some of these poems. Todd Sanders designed and printed that small volume and taught me how to fold pages and covers, measure and pound holes, bind it together with needle and thread and paste on the label. Writing the poems and making them with my own hands into something concrete and beautiful was an extraordinary experience of homage to Emily, of regaining what felt like sanity. I gave the 50 volumes produced this way to those who had been in some way especially touched by Emily's death or our loss. The same friend whose phrase "impossible loss" had seemed so right, said that these poems had touched him "in the place where every grief I've ever known in my own life is stored. I feel that somehow, and without diluting the concentration of your personal experience, you've spoken for each of us who grieves." Another friend urged me to publish the initial set of poems, thinking they'd be helpful to others who had lost the people most beloved in their lives.

For this volume I have added some poems that grew directly out of Emily's death and, in the second section, a few that concern other losses. It is my hope that my experience and what I have to say about it will be of use to others than me.

Thanks to Paul Schrading, who allowed me to use two of Barbara Schrading's woodcuts, made as part of her project, "Having Cancer is No Small Thing," initially an exhibit of woodcuts and quotations that she later made into books for her husband and sons. Thanks once again to Todd Sanders for design and publication assistance. Laurel Ellison and Anne Faigen read the manuscript carefully and made superb suggestions. Carolyn Luck gave me good advice about several of the poems. Ellie Piper, who knows the territory, gave me the title. My gratitude to my dear husband Robert Norman, and to my surviving children— Andy Norman and Marie Norman, their mates, Heidi Norman and Matt Weiss, and to our grandchildren, Katie Rose Davidson, Reece Norman, Kai Norman, Maya Weiss and Dev Weiss—is boundless. My sisters, sister-in-law, their husbands, a treasury of nephews and nieces, my dear, dear friends, members of Chatham Baroque, and Emily's other friends and associates—a much wider circle than I had the foggiest idea existed—have also extended their hands and hearts in ways that have steadied and guided me.

o

EMILY NORMAN DAVIDSON
10.10.1967—11.2.2003

PART I

Falling From Life Into Illness

title taken from a line of text by Anatole Broyard

I Don't Like Poetry

Like code,
interior, weird.
People don't talk
like that,
don't think
in those terms.
We speak prose,
say what we mean.
I would not ask
a poet for directions
nor tell a poet
my symptoms.

But then I think of
"Stopping by Woods on a Snowy Evening"
and am breathless
at woven rhyme and meter
and truth.
"The only other sound's the sweep
of easy wind and downy flake."
No prose could get that perfect
silence,
sound of unblemished snow.

There are things I want to say,
if only softly,
for few to hear,
that can't be said in prose,
at least not yet.

o

1967-2003

It's the dates,
the closed parentheses. Children
should have just one.

o

"....malignant, metastatic,
call this number on Monday,
discharged," said the doctor
she had never seen before.

She sat alone
in a bleached gown
with ties in back
on a bed
in a shocked white hospital room
where there was no one
to exclaim,
hold her hand,
question,
contest the verdict.

o

The Garden

All summer long the garden grew,
daffodils and violets, lilacs and peonies,
a field of daisies like stars on stems,
iris, roses, lavender, lilies, astilbe,
English phlox, bee balm and aster.
It was a season of illness—
annual resurrection
of spring until fall,
when everything brittled
and warblers feasted on seeds.

At times during the summer
I dug fiercely to uproot
enameled buttercups, attacked them,
nestling at the base of other flowers,
sucking their substance.

o

Keeping Watch

Exhausted of incredulity and dread,
we kept watch,
days and nights ran together,
someone said, "Go home."

So we went home to our estranged house,
in which we had lived for 35 years,
the garden haggard as cold bore down.

We let water beat us clean,
put on fresh clothes, went to the diner,
where we ordered cheese omelets,
sausage and toast for him, bacon for me.

But I wanted an order of onion rings,
hot, greasy, salty. Our daughter was dying
and what I wanted was an order of onion rings.

o

Living and Dying

1.

A month late by my calculation
but exactly right by her own—
grandparents came and went,
I taught all day, fed the other children,
too tired to have a baby—

She arrived when it suited her,
slept with hands relaxed
when she slept at all,
fretful by night.

She played with neighbor twins,
boys her age, three Irish-looking kids,
white skin, black hair, black lashes,
taken for triplets. When her older
brother and sister called
to hawks on a mountaintop,
she was wholly absorbed
in her own game,
dropping hotpads in the dirt.

I read about a witch.
In pencil drawings
the witch's hair sprang into
branches and twigs of trees.
She kept her head under covers,
looking at the pictures only
when she didn't have to listen.

At six the violin chose her.
She elbowed my ribs.
"I want to play *that*."
At ten she took off,
auditioned, made travel plans,
convinced us, out-reasoned objections,
"level-headed, bull-headed, clear-headed,"
says her friend, all these from the get-go.
She learned the world by launching herself
head first. When she lived,
a young woman alone in San Francisco,
she waltzed her car around the city,
but phoned, "How do you cook artichokes?"

2.

Her brother and sister are athletes.
We have found them, standing
apart in different playing fields,
heads back like horses, tasting the air,
same leg flexed, same hand on same hip,
wearing the same bones under their flesh.
She did too. I didn't see it
until she lost her hair.

When her sister stood on top of the world—
on a mountain in the Himalayas—
she flung her arms out in fists,
pure joy in her upflung head.
And here is a picture of Emily,
her last summer, bones full of pain,
straddling a bike, arms out, head back.
"All I want is my life the way it was."

When I weeded her garden
she came to the door,
loose black pants draped from thin hips,
white shirt, clean, elegant,
skin sheer over pulse, blue-threaded veins,
black hair, blue or green eyes, depending.
She drove a red VW bug, wore red clogs,
earrings like drops of blood.
She shopped for gowns in sales,
plucking dresses that made audiences gasp,
from racks of seedy left-overs.

I thought I could not bear
to tip that perfect body into fire.

3.

I marveled at the speed and precision
of her fingers on the neck of the violin,
the only visible effort,
the small tensing of her mouth.
What was the circuitry in her brain,
that the odd markings of ancient manuscript
could get there so fast, from seeing to doing?

She made feathery pie crust
from the recipe on the Crisco can,
apples sliced thin as leaves,
old music on the CD player,
candles on the table in a brass holder.

She hated clutter,
but let her daughter make messes
of crayons and clay on the table.

4.

For the last few nights, after she decreed
no more transfused blood,
I slept in her bed, keeping my hand against her
so she'd know I was there,
as, when she was a fractious baby
and I let her, finally at three years, cry it out,
I waked all night beside her.

At the end we kept her company.

5.

It wasn't so easy for her to die.
She made no complaint, just that
determined tensing of her mouth.

When one system shut down
another redoubled its efforts,
like giving birth, involuntary,
her body trying to save her.
She labored to breathe.
Her heart speeded up.
She ran a fever.
Her hands and feet
grew cold, abandoned
by the remnants of blood
doing their best
to keep heart and lungs going.

At the last moment her eyes sprang open—
as if for a moment amazed—
and she was gone.
What lay in her place
was nothing like her.

We dressed what was left
in red satin underwear, red earrings, red clogs,
velvet concert dress and sox that said,
"World's Best Mom" and let her go.

o

Never

"She'll never come again,
Never, never, never, never, never."
King Lear

It takes more than six "never"s
For "never" to be real.

Lear said "never" and died.
Kent praised those
who would not upon the rack
of this tough world
stretch him out longer.

Lear's rack was royalty.
It's never clear
why a man with power is loved.
Two daughters were greedy for kingdoms.
Virtuous Cordelia was, for this reason, suspect.

When I taught *Lear* one student
was beside himself. It was so unfair, needless
for Cordelia to die. No necessity of plot,
a screw-up—nothing more.

The lesson Lear learns,
limits of his power,
storm on his naked skin,
impotence of rage.
He learns of arbitrary death,
his daughter, dead because an order went wrong,

dead because a gene or cell went wrong,
some poison in soil or air,
to profit a king of industry.

She'll never come again,
never, never, never, never, never

o

Insistent from the beginning,
knew what she wanted
and how to get it,
though outranked by siblings.

In school she made a form,
Name_____ Address_____
"So you will not froget me."

As if we would. My face marred
by port wine stain, she made a sign
in crayons with flowers to the side,
"Birthmarks are beautiful
and I mean it!"

She had friends, a multitude,
more than we knew,
but liked to go off in her own company,

knew when to press her luck,
when to pull back, impatient
with indecision, wanted to go ahead
but watched out for consequences.

She was able to hear and follow,
but knew when to lead.
In an ensemble, as in marriage,
you must both follow and lead
and know when to do which.

o

It rained all day a year ago,
ending in a gold and silver sunset.
Today leaves of the Norway maple
outside my window glow gold
against wet black branches and stems,
a pewter sky. Rain falls *in memorium.*

o

Numbers

A table fit for company, my mother's gift
to her daughters. The most ordinary meal
was an occasion. She wished for bone china
but settled for cheap green plastic for everyday,
but never bread in wrappers nor jam in jars.
When we were sick we had her mother's Noritake,
with tiny pink flowers and gray leaves, on a tray
and always in a little vase a fresh bouquet.

It used to be when I set the table
for my family, I had to think how to make
the plates go round, dinner plates for adults,
salad plates for children.

"It's the numbers," says my daughter,
middle of three children,
now one of two, "They get to me."

When I set the table for the whole family—
cheerful Polish plates,
blue pattern on grey ground—
there are now enough to go around.

o

PIETER ROMBAUTS, 1706

1.

The dealer in fine instruments believed
Pieter Rombauts had made the violin.
There was a certain difference, the way
the head was shaped, narrow at top,
flared at bottom. The fiddle itself
had wide hips. Whalebone purfling
decorated and protected front and back.
All typical of Rombauts, who carried on
the work of his stepfather, Hendrik Jacobs.
Both used the same varnish.

2.

Pieter Rombauts, in his workshop:
he fashions a violin, ribs, belly,
back, joints and neck, drops
wood, maple, sycamore, spruce,
to hear how it rings; tests with his teeth
for strength. Nothing is rote. Each piece
of wood is different. He works by an open
window for light or in the dark with candles.
He measures, cuts, shapes, glues,
clamps, waits, then strings and tries
above his heart what he has made.

3.

The violin, unplayed
in a collection in Chicago,
grew brittle without vibration
of practice and performance
that wakes up wood.

I read that when the Age of Kings
ended, when heads of state rolled,
when nobility gave way to merchants,
musicians had to play to halls
large enough to seat an audience
big enough to pay the bills and needed
louder fiddles and the virtuosi
to bring in people to fill the chairs.
So earlier fiddles were remade
to be louder, showier, to withstand
greater tension. The Rombauts
was part of that history. Its neck
had been broken and lengthened,
heavier sound post, modern bridge,
steel strings. Then someone changed
course again and the Rombauts,
once old, then new, was newly old.

4.

Three hundred years
after it was made, my daughter
put Rombauts' violin against
her white neck. She liked
the sound under her ear.
In her hands it spoke and sang.
She and the first fiddler played
as one violin with two voices.

She cared for the hands that fingered
the Rombauts and drew the bow
across its sheepgut strings.
When the nurses wanted
to put needles in her hands,
she said, "No. I need my hands.
I'm a violinist."

"Keep me alive until October,"
she told them—who found veins in her arms
to put needles that took blood
and carried chemicals— "and I'll get you
tickets to the operas."

At last,
when cancer had conquered her bones,
when her marrow had stopped making blood,
when she had played for the last time,
when the famous soprano had sung
Dido's "Lament" not for her lover,
but for the dying violinist—she let them
put needles in her hands.
They lay beside her, still and bruised.

5.

She wanted the first violinist to have
her bows. I took the violin
out of the green satin bag,
saw that the varnish was worn
where it had sat against her collarbone,
the fiddle that quickened songs and dances
of long ago and far away
to now and near. Without her
to play it, it was only wood and glue.
I slid it into its green satin shroud,
cinched with silk cord,
fastened the clip that held the neck,
shut case, zipped cover,
sent the Rombauts back to the dealer
in fine instruments—and wept.

o

GRAND CANYON

In 1869 a war hero with one arm
explored the length of Green River,
its water clear from Wyoming
until it met the silty Colorado.
"Too thick to drink, too thin to plow,"
his party said. John Wesley Powell
believed river had cut canyon
as volcanic pressure thrust the plateau up.

My father was right: the Grand Canyon
was exteme erosion.
A boy, he hiked to the bottom,
on the way out carried rocks
in his wood and canvas backpack,
80 pounds worth, made
a diagram in his journal
of geologic history he'd carried.
Later he wrote of soil,
wind and water and lichen on rock,
eons of wear and tear,
held to the earth by vegetation.

Grazing clipped away plants,
rains mined away soil,
dumping mud and rocks in streams
and valleys and towns below.
He grieved the tragedy—hubris of herders,
who thought that land was free.

I live at the edge of the Grand Canyon.
It's night. I know the hole is there:
at midnight I feel a darker blackness,
carved away by the river that empties
at last into the Gulf.

I know that kind hands would
reach out to guide me back
from the edge if they knew where I am,
alone with the smell of ponderosa pine
and the hauntings of nocturnal creatures.

I don't want to explore this hole.
I don't want to be here,
alone with the echo of the one-armed man
and the memory of my father,
lugging rocks up from the bottom.

It is magnificent by day
in the clear air. But to know this void
I have to go to the bottom, touch
the river that flows to the Gulf.

o

Underground Streams

I walk along streets.
They've always been there,
concrete, permanent. Sometimes
in the shopping area I wonder,
what used to on that corner
before Boston Chicken
or the arrogant new drugstore
that was, for years, a weedy lot.
You forget the past.

Underneath these streets, they say,
run rivers and creeks, tributaries
to the Monongahela, Allegheny and Ohio,
perhaps marshes, wetlands.

The Indians knew
springy trails underfoot,
along the waterways.
Then came intruders, seeking land,
a fort, control of the Ohio,
the way west.

As city grew out from fort,
they paved over inconvenient streams.
Streets seem strong and fixed,
but underneath run rivers.

I think we are evolved
to survive loss. Otherwise, what?
We go on. There are things
to be done: making ends meet,
groceries, laundry,
bills, birthdays, grandchildren,
the garden, this, that. I go on.
But often, during the day,
I hear those rivers that run
below us and drown.

o

Raking Leaves

Who would have thought one tree—
old Norway maple, wounded
by lightning and disease, big branches
broken off, lopsided this time of year—
would have so many leaves? In summer
they shade the backyard, a cool haven
for squirrels and birds, too. Then a time
of gold, too short, before the wind rips
what remains and covers green plants
with brown paving. Today I raked
the leaves on the path, crisp on top with ice,
sodden underneath, and carried them
to the compost. I had it in mind that decay,
like layers of dinosaur bones and ancient ferns,
would stew all winter into hydrocarbons
and I would find diamonds or coal
next summer to dress emerging plants.
It is consolation to think of mingling
dead matter, once so green and gold,
in an earth that goes on and on.

o

These are things I know about eternity.

It's not a place where angels in robes
gather on clouds, flap wings and play on harps
for something to do. Think of all those centuries of death!
Where in some eternal place would all souls fit,
even with a good supply of architects?

Eternity is you. You recapitulate
your mother, translucent skin,
pointed chin, big eyes, same funny bone and focus,
knowing what you want.
I see your father in you, too, the sideways look,
storehouse of information.
This was her bequest, the convergence
of genes no mere god could engineer.

One man wrote, "Deeply troubled
by the wrong order, somehow,
of your daughter's death, I turn
to the wonderful Chatham Baroque CDs,
whose music makes it seem that the world
will go on in good order forever."
One friend writes that she has taken
your mother's spirit into herself,
a kind of eucharist, and can better help
the broken, the troubled, the fearful
trying to mend their lives.

Some have heard her spirit
in the splendid baroque guitar her colleague plays,
modeled on one built four centuries ago.
The guitarist thinks she left her talent
to the trio that survives her.
He says he can play passages
he couldn't before her death.

I cannot answer the question of eternity
for others, only for myself.
We have no proof of anything, only experience.

o

"What would you think ..."

she said, near the end, when it was clear she wouldn't live,
"of putting a small boulder in your backyard garden
with my name on it—lower case letters—
and maybe Dad could make a bench
to sit on in summer."

The backyard is sheltered by an elderly maple,
shading violets dug up from her house, ferns, columbine,
red roses with yellow centers that love shade.
And on the day before Easter
we put her ashes under the small boulder
with her name on it—
only partly lower case—
each throwing a trowel-full of dirt on top
before we rolled the rock into place.

I planted helleborus for late winter blooms.
And every morning I go out and say to the rock,
"Hi, Honey," and tell her the news.

o

Aubade

Our naked bodies, honeyed
in warmth of sleep.
I think of rose-colored hills
in high desert
storing morning sun.
Outside our window birds
are ecstatic, and light leaks
in around the shades.
We drowse and touch a greeting.
"It's so sad without Emmy," he says.

o

The Ring

There was contention between us about it,
a rose gold band with small sapphire set
in yellow gold, handcrafted, unusual.
I fell in love with it.
As such things go, it didn't cost a lot,
but he said my wanting it was greedy.
So I bought it myself and wore it,
away from my wedding ring,
on the other hand.
It was a sign that in marriage
there is yet separation.
But when our daughter was dying,
I put the ring
next to my wedding band.
I needed the rings together
on my aging hand.

o

THE GUEST

A fever of preparation,
practical things,
clean towels and sheets,
new box of tissues,
bedtime reading on shelves,
bathroom spit and polished,
toothbrush glass,
all in readiness.

Then everything changes.
The house, possessed, no longer ours,
to run to the bathroom naked at night,
to pick a fight,
to track mud in from the garden,
to leave the paper on the breakfast table,
folded more or less.

The guest commandeers
our whole house,
new sounds and habits,
leaves toothbrush and comb where they fall,
uses the razor I shave my legs with.
We watch our tongues and tiptoe
to the bathroom wearing robes.

The guest has a key, comes in quietly,
sleeps late, retreats by day, door closed.
We go about our lives,
rake dried leaves out of the garden,
take up delayed projects,
those that had staled
when this fathomless presence was new.

Every now and again, when I have forgotten
that there is a guest at all,
grief emerges from that closed room
and declares itself.

o

Old Tree

The Norway maple towers higher than our house
and shades two full backyards.
It has been knocked about, hit twice by lightning,
oozing wounds, shedding branches in every wind.
Even so it's playground to squirrels
who race corkscrew up the trunk and launch,
tails floating, from the smallest branches.

The topmost limb, wrenched, amputated,
dropped on our ferns and hostas
in a microburst, a vertical tornado,
that knocked out power and sailed
peach and lime blossoms of a tulip tree
from another part of town
into our backyard.

After a long, gray winter
a pair of red-bellied woodpeckers
found or made a hole
in the skyward stump.
The male, in his brilliant cap and cape,
cleaned out the hole, tossing scraps
of rotten wood like snow.
His mate, carmined at the nape,
sat, scarlet-capped, in the hole,
scattering the occasional beakfull of chips,
sometimes taking a break along the branch.

We followed the tree-top drama
of nesting and what we took to be
laying of eggs and care of chicks
as a sign. We watched
with naked eyes and binoculars
and read in bird books.
The neighbors were drawn in.

Then came starlings, harassing
the nesting woodpecker,
a coordinated attack, three against one,
driving the woodpeckers away,
and took the hole for themselves.

We mourned the family of hopeful woodpeckers.
Leaves soon screened the starlings
and their stolen lodging from view.
A neighbor says a red tailed hawk lives nearby,
even in this urban neighborhood,
and has carried off one of the squirrels,
aerial acrobats of our old tree.

o

The Duration of Grief

She is everywhere:
cobalt bowl with white rabbit,
loping in moonlight,
clear amber earrings,
brought back from a tour in Mexico,
saved e-mail messages,
people—so many—
who ask "How are you?
How's Katie?"

It's not that we forget,
not likely! He says
he doesn't revel in the danger
of his power tools now.
I write verse, postponing prose.

And yet, on Mother's Day,
I was—again—startled.
How could it be
that my child had died
of a disease other people get?

o

MILKY WAY

I've heard that Earth is part of the Milky Way.
On a clear night you can see
what must be our neighbors, other stars
scattered like brilliants across a black sky.
When I look around me, I see no sparkling planets,
only—only?— miracle of trees
flushing green in spring,
tips of new plants where last year's died.

But there are gray days, clouded over.
The night sky is opaque. I can see
nothing farther than my hand, covered
with liver spots and wrinkled skin.
It's hard to think of being on a planet
that rotates among others
when hurt makes me singular,
when I feel solitary in the universe,
when I, me, my crowd out all others.

There *are* others, some I know, more not,
who have lost children, and I think
the world revolves on an axis of sorrow.
But maybe we are held together in a
magnetic field, like the stars
in a constellation or a galaxy.

The *New York Times*, "Science" section, says
that disasters like earthquakes and tsunamis,
shifting of earth's tectonic plates,
are part of the earth's resilience,
refashioning ecologies.

o

PRAYER

Believers pray for daily bread.
The world seems nourished by grief.
It is the other side of love.

o

PART II

Can You See the Stars in the Daytime from the Bottom of a Well?

Avalanche

Lincoln Ellison
August 2, 1908—March 9, 1958

He went out the door happy,
a perfect day ahead on skis,
away from wrangling traffic
of work and endless minutiae
of those he loved. Free
in cold air, a clean fall
of snow, his strong limbs stretching
and men to share breaking
of trail and lunch in trees
just off John Paul Jones Ridge.

He had tried for religion,
but pre-Copernican preachers
constructing the universe
after their limited
imaginations recoiled.
Miracles of order,
variation, intricacy,
basilicas of timber,
masses of birdsong,
silence full of sound,
and slow abruptions
pushed the land around.

Alone he joined
what he believed in.
He started out of trees,
breaking trail, ahead of the others,

triggered the rush of newfallen snow
that hung from underlying ice
and swept him away, smothered him
in perfect silence. His companions,
not seeing ski tracks, knew
what had happened and searched
and when they found him
it was too late to take him out.

He lay in state
on a bier of snow, watched
by clear mountain stars
as he'd have liked,
before the company of mourners
tried to make sense of it.

An abrupt end to a lean and vigorous life,
but my father stayed with his daughters—
recombinant grandchildren
he never met,
ways we could think,
classics of ecology,
"Our Weight in the Balance of Nature,"
the tall tales he told.

Steep hillsides shed avalanches.
He was reclaimed by the way the world works.
Whatever panic and brief regret he felt,
he was at home with his last breath.

o

Two Kinds of Death

Laurel Elizabeth Elver Ellison Everett
April 29, 1909—September 26, 2002

She was ready to die, but held on.
The nun asked my sisters, "Is one of you not here?
Have her tell your mother it's OK to die."
I did, weeping a continent away.
My sisters swear that, phone to her ear,
tears slid down her cheeks, she smiled,
as she had not for years, and died.

                          Before her funeral,
around the kitchen table, we went through photo albums.
There was a sod house, a surround of prairie,
    one room school,
her father homesteading, Wisconsin, Iowa,
    Colorado, California,
mayor/doctor/lawyer/preacher in towns he set in motion,
a fierce-eyed German, fourteenth of fifteen
    with an improbable name,
Leonard Charles Fritz Frances Elver,
    whose brothers taught him
to swim by throwing him overboard. Patient Nelly Bartell,
bore him children, a son, my mother, two who died young.
Mother told of playing out of doors, a girl in Colorado,
taking a stick to beat on rocks to scare away rattlesnakes.

She played piano for weddings and funerals
    at her father's church,
slender, glowing, curly chestnut hair, brought up right
    by faith-healing father
and a mother who disapproved of sewing doll clothes
    on the Sabbath.
She learned how to teach young children at UCLA,
where she met Lincoln, handsome botanist,
    who loved to swim
naked at night in the Pacific, wrote bad poetry,
    took her to Montana plains
to a wooden shack at Hogback Wells, dead ringer
    for the prairie house,
took her skiing at Christmas to sleep on bedded boughs
    in a snow cave.

She knew the arts of housewifery, canned the fruits
    of Victory Garden,
Queen Ann cherries from our massive tree, churned butter
from cow's cream, taught me to play piano, braiding
    my hair
while I practiced. She taught me to hang laundry, pinning
shirts along yoke seams, sheets with corners matched
for easy folding, socks pinned by toes, ready to roll up.
When my teacher urged a book, then worried about
    two characters,
living together unwed, I told her—proud—
my mother had nothing to do with my reading.

After my father died, she invited a friend from childhood
for Christmas. His wife, too, had died and both were lonely.
They lived in the farm town where she was first
preacher's kid, then rancher's wife. Childless,
he took on her four daughters, their four husbands.
When he died, eleven grandchildren,
    one great granddaughter.

Ninety three years of sturdy health. For over a score
dementia gathered, tangling the mind
that looked out on California hills, gold and amethyst,
and saw white bark of quaking aspen, black-green fir.
She thought confusion meant she had moved,
just as she'd done so often, put dishes the dogs had licked
in cupboard rather than dishwasher.
Sociable instincts the last to go, she conversed in nonsense
as if it were English, later found visitors alarming,
grew thin as a mad Russian princess,
    burning eyes like her father's,
aristocratic face framed by white waves of hair.

The last time I saw her, she lived in sleep.
I brushed her silver hair, stroked her arm,
told her I loved her, left in tears.

When she was my mother and together we passed
a nursing home, whose inmates sagged in front of TV,
she said, "If I'm ever like that, take me out and shoot me."

o

Can You See the Stars in Daytime
From the Bottom of a Well?

Barbara Schrading
1936—1997

1.

It was an astonishing request:
"Will you help me find a way to die?"

2.

She fell into a well: pain, severe, constant, inexplicable.
"Isolating," she said, a turning inward against
what hurt—herself.
She found comfort in scripture, communion,
a fragile shield against exhausting fear.
Diagnosis was a death sentence,
the eating away of bone, learning to live
in her dining room, her family, the world outside,
never knowing when.

But she lived seven good years, interrupted
by bouts of worsening,
savoring places, children, a brood of grandchildren, food,
keeping a journal, drawing, making woodcuts,
"Having Cancer Is No Small Thing."

At the bottom of the well there was a kind of night.
She searched for handholds, found none.
But in the darkness, even in daytime, she saw stars,

3.

When she asked me for help, too many bones were broken
for her to manage a phone book, even a phone.
She would not implicate husband and sons,
but would tell them.
I found a doctor and lawyer to advise.
The best way, they said,
was not to eat or drink.
It would not take long
nor cause pain.

At the end, she said "thank you."
She died alone at night.

o

Maybe I Do Like Poetry After All

The words I found
drilled deep
and allowed me
to go on living.

o

COLOPHON

Text for this book was set in Adobe Jenson
and printed by Thomson-Shore Inc. of Dexter, Michigan

SMOKE AND
MIRRORS PRESS